THE

FORE-ARM ROTATION PRINCIPLE

IN PIANOFORTE PLAYING

ITS APPLICATION AND MASTERY

BY

TOBIAS MATTHAY

(Professor, Lecturer and Fellow of the Royal Academy of Music, and Founder of the
Tobias Matthay Pianoforte School, London, etc.)

Read & Co.

Copyright © 2021 Read & Co. Books

This edition is published by Read & Co. Books,
an imprint of Read & Co.

This book is copyright and may not be reproduced or copied in any
way without the express permission of the publisher in writing.

British Library Cataloguing-in-Publication Data
A catalogue record for this book is available
from the British Library.

Read & Co. is part of Read Books Ltd.
For more information visit
www.readandcobooks.co.uk

Tobias Matthay

Tobias Augustus Matthay was born on 19th February 1858, in Clapham, Surrey, England. He was an English pianist, teacher and composer.

Matthay's parents originally came from northern Germany and eventually became naturalised British subjects. He studied composition at the 'Royal Academy of Music' (London) under Sir William Sterndale Bennett and Arthur Sullivan, and piano with William Dorrell and Walter Macfarren. Matthay served as a sub-professor there from 1876 to 1880, and became an assistant professor of pianoforte in 1880, before being promoted to professor in 1884.

Alongside Frederick Corder and John Blackwood McEwen (both composers and music teachers), he founded the Society of British Composers in 1905. This organisation was established with the aim of protecting the interests of British composers and to provide publication, promotion and performance opportunities. It was disbanded thirteen years later, in 1918. Matthay remained at the Royal Academy of Music until 1925, when he was forced to resign because McEwen – his former student who was then the Academy's Principal – publicly attacked his teaching.

In 1903, after over a decade of observation, analysis, and experimentation, Matthay published *The Act of Touch*, an encyclopaedic volume that influenced piano pedagogy throughout the English-speaking world. So many students were soon in quest of his insights that two years later he opened the Tobias Matthay Pianoforte School, first in Oxford Street, then in 1909 relocating to Wimpole Street, where it remained for the next thirty years. He soon became known for his teaching principles that stressed proper piano touch and analysis of arm movements. He wrote several additional books on piano technique that brought him international recognition, and in 1912 he published *Musical Interpretation*, a widely read book that analyzed the principles of effective musicianship.

Many of Matthay's pupils went on to define a school of twentieth century English pianism, including York Bowen, Myra Hess, Clifford Curzon, Moura Lympany, Eunice Norton, Lytle Powell, Irene Scharrer, Lilias Mackinnon, Guy Jonson, Vivian Langrish and Harriet Cohen. He was also the teacher of Canadian pianist Harry Dean, English composer Arnold Bax and English conductor Ernest Read.

In his private life, Matthay married Jessie (née Kennedy) in 1893, the sister of Marjory Kennedy-Fraser (the Scottish singer, composer and arranger). She sadly died in 1937.

Tobias Matthay died at his country home, High Marley, near Haslemere, on 15th December 1945. He was eighty-seven years old.

FOREWORD

As the function of the rotary adjustments of the forearm has been made clear in my various works on Technique, very few words are here required.*

The principle of the exertion and relaxation of the muscles which twist and un-twist the Forearm upon itself is probably more far-reaching than any other of the fundamental principles of Technique. Whether we describe this function of the forearm (accompanied by movement or not) as *rotary* or "rocking," "rolling," "twisting," or "oscillating," the term is immaterial, but its comprehension and application are vital.

The proper application of this rotary principle will help us in every note we play, while its improper application will as inevitably hinder us at every point.†

Again, since the fifth finger, for instance, is obviously rendered helpless when the direction of the rotary exertion is downwards at the thumb-side of the hand, it follows, that to give the fifth finger sufficient *basis* for its operation against the key, we must *omit* the rotary exertion which was previously used to help the thumb. Hence we find, that the supposed weakness (i. e., disablement) of the fifth and fourth fingers is mainly due to the *wrong* rotary exertions of the Forearm, and that these fingers become practically as "strong" as the others the moment the rotary exertions are reversed in their favour.‡ When playing a *single* (not "broken") octave these adjustments must be nicely balanced so as to equalize the thumb and fifth. But the remaining fingers are also just as much in need of such help from the forearm, rotatively, as the thumb and fifth. It is easy to decide in every case whether it is a twisting or untwisting action of the forearm which is required, for this depends strictly on the *order*, or *succession* in which the fingers enter into play—that is: allowing the finger last used to serve as a pivot, the direction of the momentary rotary exertion for the next finger is away from (or upwards from) that last note, and is towards (or downwards to) the note and finger about to be used.

These exertions of the forearm on its axis, moreover, whether properly or wrongly applied, do not necessarily betray their existence by external signs of rotary *movement;* on the contrary, such movements are not often required. In some instances, however, such movements are desirable in playing; while they are invaluable in the learning stage. When no actual or noticeable movement accompanies such exertions, this means that these exertions are in this case perfectly balanced by the exertions of the fingers against the keys. We should also note, that in Touches requiring lapse of Arm-weight during key-descent, such weight is distributed to the involved fingers by the rotary exertion; while in Touches not requiring *individually*-applied Weight-lapse for each note, the same rotary-exertion principle (in conjunction with the *inertia* of the *self-supported* arm) still helps to provide the fingers with the basis for their action of depressing the keys.

---

* See "*Act of Touch,*" "*First Principles,*" and especially "*Some Commentaries on Technique*" (Longmans, Green and Co.). Also, "*Relaxation Studies*" (Bosworth and Co.,) and, "*The Child's First Steps*" (Joseph Williams and Boston Music Co.).

† For instance, if we fully relax the rotation-muscles of the forearm, the hand will roll over to its side, thumb upwards. To turn the hand into its playing-position (palm downwards) we are therefore compelled to exert (or energize) the muscles which twist the forearm upon itself, i. e., we must *rotate* it upon itself for one quarter of an arc. Again, to keep the hand in the playing-position thus gained, the same muscles must *continue* active in some measure, although the effort is so slight that it should be difficult to recognize its presence,—it should not be perceptible indeed *unless something outside* is opposed to this rotary effort—for instance, the Piano-key. Further we find, that to apply the thumb against the keys with any effect (beyond *ppp* tone-amount) we must, to help the thumb during the act of key-depression, *increase* the energy supplied by this same rotary-exertion, although such *exertion* may remain unaccompanied by any actual movement rotatively.

‡ If we use *both* sets of exertions (towards thumb *and* towards fifth) we of course "set" or stiffen the forearm rotatively. We are always prone to fall into this error, and to ruin all our technique by such tug-of-war between these two opposite exertions, in place of the neat little forearm *twists*, either reiterated or alternate, which are required as we progress from note to note.

In effect, we see that it is practically impossible to play any note on the piano without the intervention of this ever-present principle, element or function, and that no passage can be given with ease unless we accurately time and supply the requisite changes, reversals, or repetitions of this rotary action with proper freedom and power—these reversals, or repetitions, invariably following the direction of the *succession* of the fingers on the keyboard.*

We see then how supremely important it is that this fundamental although simple matter should be thoroughly understood, even by the beginner; and to render its immediate application easier, the following *steps* are given for its mastery. These "Steps" should be studied, each one, in the order given, and with ample experiments at the instrument, etc., in each case. It is of no use merely reading through this brochure.†

---

* Owing to its not necessarily exhibiting any movement, the older teachers entirely overlooked the true nature of this principle, although many of them showed (by the material they provided for practice) that they were *unconsciously* aware of its influence; for instance, CHARLES CZERNY, in his admirable " Fingerfertigkeit," etc. Nevertheless, some later teachers have recognized its influence more specifically, only however when accompanied by *Movement;* that is to say, where notes are played alternately by the extreme fingers; hence arose the term " Seitenschlag." Still more recent teachers (owing to their still trying to rely on ocular demonstrations alone) have gone to the opposite extreme, and are actually doing harm in the meantime, by wildly asserting that rotary *movements* (" Rollung ") can supplant all finger-action and movement!—thus propagating one of the worst fallacies of so many which have arisen with regard to Piano Touch.

† The author's " *Child's First Steps in Piano-Playing* " shows how this vital matter is to be brought to the knowledge of the young. The course there given can also be followed with advantage by the adult beginner. The study of the Rotation Principle should indeed begin practically with the pupil's very first attempts at Pianoforte playing.

TOBIAS MATTHAY

HASLEMERE, SURREY
August, 1911

THE
FORE–ARM ROTATION PRINCIPLE

Step I: *Preparatory*—away from the keyboard.

a) Allow your arm to fall lightly and limply upon your knee. Be sure to leave it quite free. It will then fall with the hand *sideways*—with the thumb-side of your hand *upwards.**

b) Let it lie thus loosely for a moment, and then raise your arm a foot or so, with the hand remaining in this sideways position.

c) Now turn the hand freely until the palm is downwards—the knuckles up.

d) Note that this *partial rotation* of the hand and forearm is caused by an almost imperceptible exertion of the muscles which twist the forearm upon itself, and that this almost unnoticeable "twisting" (or rotary) exertion also serves to retain the hand in its playing-position: i. e., it is this gentle exertion of the forearm, rotatively, which keeps your hand turned knuckles upwards, and if you cease this exertion completely, the hand will untwist, back to the sideway position. Test this again and again.

Having learnt this important fact about the hand and arm, rotatively, take the next Step:—

Step II: *a)* Hold one hand extended, with palm open and turned upwards: lay the other hand sideways (thumb up) upon the middle phalange of the extended fingers of the other hand. See Fig. 1.

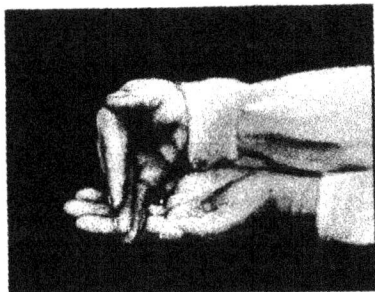

Fig. 1.

* Only in this position can the Forearm Rotation-muscles be completely at rest—relaxed.

b) Now roll (rotate or twist) this lying hand so as to hit into the palm of the extended one, and so as to cause a sharp "clap." Practise this until you can do it quite easily.†

c) Practise the other hand in the same way.

d) Now reverse the exercise, by rolling upon the *thumb*-side of the lying hand—instead of the little finger-side as before. See Fig. 2.

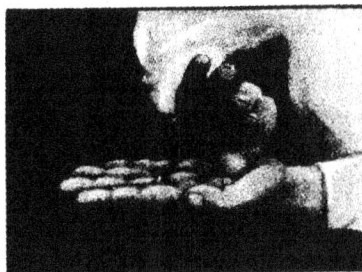

Fig. 2.

The ball of its thumb now rests on the wrist-end of the extended hand and you clap towards the little-finger side. This seems more difficult to do than the last, not because it is really more difficult muscularly, but because we cannot at once learn to roll the little-finger side of the hand *upwards* (upon the thumb) without "stiffening." Insist, however, on practising this exercise until you can avoid thus using the *wrong (or opposite) exertion* implied by such "stiffening."

e) Practise this form of the exercise with the other hand.

f) Combine both forms of the exercise, by alternately clapping with the thumb-side of the hand, and then with the little-finger side of it. Thus:— let the thumb-side rise, and then moving it down sharply, "clap" into the palm of the supporting

† Be sure that the force used is from the *Forearm* only. Do not allow a twisting of the *whole* arm (from the shoulder) to help in this clapping.

Whole arm rotation is rarely required except for extreme *fortes*. The difficulty is to learn to give the required exertion only by *forearm* twist.

hand, and follow this, by letting the fifth-finger side rise, and then giving a "clap" with that.

NOTE. A simpler form of preparatory exercise is to lay the hand upon a table, etc., and to execute the indicated motions upon it.

A large number of additional preparatory and advanced "rotation" exercises are found in Set IV of the author's "*Relaxation Studies*" (Bosworth and Co.).

Step III: *At the keyboard*—Place the hand sideways, with the tip of the little finger (sideways also) on a key. Rest very gently on this key—with no more weight than is just sufficient to keep it depressed. Now, just as in the previous "clapping" exercise, roll the hand and forearm round so as to bring the thumb swiftly (but quite gently) upon a note *a fifth distant* from the little finger's note. Do this so gently and neatly as not to sound that note at all. Repeat this rotary swing-down *to* the key, until you can do this with perfect freedom and *neatness*, and can even take hold *upon* this key with the thumb—with a neat little pressure—but still without depressing or sounding the note.

Step IV: Repeat the last exercise, but now, when you reach the key, increase the rotary-*exertion* (and thumb *exertion*) sufficiently to enable the thumb to take the key down and to sound it. Do this quite softly at first, and louder afterwards.

NOTE. Remember, all tone-producing exertions must be applied only during *the descent of the key* and must *cease* the moment sound is reached in Key-descent. Therefore *time* them accurately, so that you do not apply the force too late to make the required tone; also *time* them accurately so that the free swing-down *to* the key, and the more forceful movement *down with the key* may form one unbroken swing downwards—increasing in its energy to the last moment.

It may be well here shortly to sum up the laws of key-treatment:—I) Remember, sound depends solely on the *kind of motion* you give to the key during its descent—the quicker the speed the louder is the tone, and the more gradually you attain this *motion* the more beautiful and under control is the tone. II) Remember to *feel* the resistance the key offers before, and during, its descent—it varies exactly with the tone, and it is the only way you can *guide* the tone with surety; and meanwhile do all you have to do *before* the key is down, since you cannot alter the tone after that. III) Remember accurately to *mean* every sound both as to *time* and *tone*, and be sure to *listen* to the actual sound. Listen, so that you may not waste energy after it is too late (in key descent) to make sound; and listen also, so that you may let the key *rise* always at the right moment to stop the sound—an instantaneous rebound of the key, if you wish *Staccato*. These matters are fully elucidated in the author's earlier works; *See* Note, page 3.

Step V: You must now repeat the last two Steps (*III* and *IV*) but now use the *thumb* as a pivot in place of the fifth finger. Rest upon the thumb now, but do so just as lightly as you did before with the fifth finger. Freely tilt the hand up at the fifth finger side as much as you can without in the least forcing the action.

NOTE. If necessary, at first keep the elbow well away from the body—such "outward" position of it renders rotation towards the thumb easier.

From this position (with the fifth finger side of the hand tilted upwards) let that side of the hand now roll down till the fifth finger is brought into contact with its key, but without depressing it. After this has been learnt, again (as in *Step IV*) let this gentle fall upon the key be continued unbrokenly by that further movement, *with the key*, which gives the sound.

NOTE. Remember, the necessary Weight and Muscular force must be *added* at the right moment; that is, you must *exert* the fifth finger (and also the forearm, rotarily, to help it) *after* the key has been reached, but *before* the key has reached the bed beneath it; and the amount of the force and weight you apply must always be strictly in answer to the resistance you feel the key offers at its surface-level and during its descent.

Step VI: Next make this into a rhythmical exercise, thus:

Ex. 1.

Left hand two octaves lower; hands practised separately at first.

Be sure to *cease* all the tone-making energy the moment you hear the sound of the *forte* note; and for the sake of the *Tenuto* you must leave only just sufficient Weight that will serve to keep the key depressed.

To test this, change the passage somewhat, by playing the *loud* note Staccato, (as in Ex. 4), but do not allow the *staccato*-finger to leave the surface of its key. That is, time all force and weight to cease, so that the key may be free to *rebound*. If you succeed in this, the key will carry up with it the finger and the hand, lying loosely upon it.

NOTE. A further *test* for this very necessary freedom, *is to move the hand freely up and down* several times, while holding down each note in turn, for you are bound to omit the objectionable *down*-arm exertion, if you try freely to raise and lower the *knuckles* while holding a note down. And you thus ensure holding that note freely. *See* page 106 "*Relaxation Studies*."

Practise the left hand similarly.

Later on, change the form of the exercise to the following :—

Ex. 2.

NOTE. Remember, that in playing these repeated notes, each one requires a *repetition* of the *same* slight rotary exertion—either towards the fifth finger or towards the thumb.

Step VII: You must next learn to apply this "rotary" help to *all* the fingers in turn. Proceed exactly as in Step *V* and *VI*, but on the following notes, (Ex. 3) :

Ex. 3.

Also, later on, test for accuracy in tone-production (as in Step *VI*), by allowing the second note to be a true (key-rebounding) Staccato, being careful that the staccato is purely the result of accurately-*ceased* action, and without any "*pulling-up*" of finger or hand. Practise the hands *separately all this time.*

Step VIII: Now try to learn to play the hands together. Do this in the (muscularly) easier way first, by taking the physical *rotary-adjustments* by *similar* motion—when the musical (note) progression will of course be by contrary motion. *See* Ex. 4.

Ex. 4.

* Left hand, two octaves lower.

Later on, learn to play passages which are *musically* in similar motion—in which case of course you require the opposite Rotary exertions and relaxations in the two hands.

NOTE. Unless you thoroughly realize that the *opposite* rotary exertions are required of the two hands and arms, when you play sounds in succession by similar motion, a conflict of exertions will sympathetically occur in *both* limbs. That is, *both* sets of forearm rotation-muscles will then come into operation, and will to that extent hamper your playing. It is well therefore here to take some *preliminary* Exercises first, away from the Piano. As good an exercise as any is merely to hold your arms out in front of you, and to turn the hands round alternately from right to left, and from left to right, but being most careful to do this with perfect freedom. *See* also: "*A Child's First Steps*," and the many preliminary and other Rotation exercises provided in "*Relaxation Studies*."

Step IX: You have already learnt during the last Steps to give this rotary-help to two adjacent fingers in succession—to the Thumb and Index, and to the Little finger and Ring finger. It now only remains to establish this association, muscularly, between the remaining fingers: that is, between 4–3, and 3–2. When you have done this, you can then start work on "five-finger exercises." For this purpose, practise the following :—

Ex. 5.

Also, as in previous Steps, practise the second note (the forte note) *staccato*, to ensure accuracy in "aiming" the tone.

Step X: You must now learn to practise a five-finger exercise correctly. Here remember to think each successive note as a *progression* from the note last played,—a progression *musically* and *rotatively* thus :—

Ex. 6.

You may sound each note strongly, but you must hold it quite lightly. You therefore *progress*, muscularly, from a very light *action* to a *strong* one each time; that is, from a *light* holding finger (however strongly the note was sounded) to a *strong*-sounding finger. Moreover, you must also always think the passage as having rhythmical landmarks — for instance, *from C towards G*, and again *from G towards C*.

In the early stages, it is indeed best to re-enforce this idea, by actually stopping on the last of the five notes each time, thus making the exercise into a very short phrase, as shown in the example.

Step XI: Next, you must learn to determine in which *direction* to give these little rotary jerks, which thus help *every* finger whatever the nature of the passage.

When you play the *first* note of a phrase, the direction of the rotary impulse is determined by which side of the hand your finger belongs to — either fifth finger side or thumb side. But in all *subsequent* notes of a phrase the finger last used acts as a pivot, and the direction of the rotary-impulse for each successive finger then depends on its position relatively to this preceding pivot-finger. Thus, when you play the middle finger *after the thumb*, the rotation-exertion is towards the little finger side of the hand; whereas, when you play the middle finger *after the little finger* the rotation is the reverse — towards the thumb side of the hand. It is always a twist towards the side of the hand to which the playing finger belongs.*

This is a most important rule, and has hardly any exceptions. An exception is, when you turn a *long* finger over a short one, in passages of double notes, such as double-notes scales, etc. Also, when turning a finger for a *large* extension over the thumb, the rule may possibly be reversed. But in all other cases the rule applies unaltered. For instance, in the scale and arpeggio, when you turn a finger over the thumb, the *rotary-twist* for that finger is towards the *little finger* side of the hand, not towards the thumb side, as one would at first imagine.

Step XII: After learning to play Scales, you must attempt the Arpeggio. Here you should prepare yourself by practising the "group" first. Now this "group" forms one of the best "rotation" exercises which can be devised.

It should take the form of Ex. 7.

Practise these groups in all keys, major and minor. Notice that the notes (and fingers) used as "pivots" are here to be played *piano* and that these are held down, whereas the alternate notes are played *forte*, and *staccato* also. This helps to strengthen the idea of *progression* — which, remember, is always to be *from* a light action *towards* a stronger action. This also helps to eradicate that constant temptation to waste force on the keybeds, and therefore makes for *accuracy* in applying force for key-depression — for tone therefore — and for *musical* accuracy therefore.

The "held notes" should be held so freely as to allow a free up-and-down movement of the *knuckles* as a test for this *freedom*.†

Step XIII: These groups may with advantage be modified for the advanced player in the ways shown on the next page. Practise all keys :—

Ex. 7.

---

* Remember, the exertion " towards " the required finger must *not* take the form of a *horizontal* (side-ways) jerk, on the contrary the exertion of the forearm must always be purely a rotary one, and the opposite exertion must carefully be omitted.
† See Note to Step VI.

Ex. 8.

(a)

(b)

With addition of the extension element, and with rotation-accents given at alternate sides of the hand :—

Ex. 9.

etc.

etc.

With the addition of repeated notes :—

Ex. 10.

etc.

* The left hand to be played two octaves lower.

With still more searching extensions :—

Ex. 11.

etc.

Practise such extreme extensions with great caution—always with perfect freedom, otherwise they will prove harmful instead of useful.

With "contractions" thus :—

Ex. 12.

Step XIV : Finally, *analyse* every passage you play (whether apparently simple or the reverse) into its component Rotary-adjustments, from note to note. Constantly recur to such analytical study of the Rotation-element in every passage, however familiar the piece. Much bad practice and much good time will thus be saved. Also practise Studies particularly suggestive of such rotary-changes. For instance some of Czerny's " Finger-fertigkeit."*

The advanced and *musical* player and artist will find excellent material for such Rotary-study, even in those most musical of all " Studies"— Chopin's. The great one in *A* minor — Op. 25, No. 11 — is perhaps one of the best technical studies ever invented for rotational purposes. The *G* flat of Op. 10 and the *C* minor of Op. 25 are also much to the point.

But do not fail analytically to decide the "rotation" stresses for each note before practice. For instance, taking the last mentioned Study :—

Ex. 13.

In the right hand the rotation-help is here required towards the thumb-side of the hand for the *first* note, this is followed by two rotary jerks towards little finger-side of the hand to help the *index* and *little* fingers, then one again towards the thumb-side of the hand to help the thumb; whereas for the left hand these actions are precisely the reverse ones. Hence the difficulty of playing this wonderful piece with success, technically, and without fatigue.

Passages in *double-notes* should also thus be analysed, and the passages practised *brokenly ;* also giving them broken both upwards and downwards, so as to practise the rotations alternately for both sides of the hand. For instance, Henselt's " Si oiseau jétais " :— *See* Ex. 14.

"Double-thirds" scales also offer excellent ground for practice of this nature. They should be practised while giving close attention to rotary-freedom and often studied brokenly on the same *principle* as shown in Ex. 14.†

Ex. 14.

* Particularly for this purpose, Nos. 4, 7, 8, 11, and also Nos. 15, 16, 19, 20, 22, 24, 35, 41, 43 and 44. Also, No. 34 for the " holding finger" Test Ex. *See* Note to Step VI, page 7. Remember, it is not a question of rotary movements, but of *exertions*, mostly invisible.
† See (by same author) " Double-Third Scales, their fingering and practice "—" *Practice-Card*," No. I: The T. M. P. S. Edition, (Joseph Williams and Boston Music Co.).

APPENDIX

Note No. I — A MOST SUGGESTIVE EXPERIMENTAL EXERCISE:

To make clear the function and application of the rotation muscles, perhaps the most convincing experiment of all is as follows:—

Gently and yet firmly press together all the fingers — leaving them in a more or less bent position.

Rest this solid mass of fingers upon two adjacent black keys, allowing two of the protruding finger tips to touch these two keys.

Now sound these two notes alternately by means of a gentle continuous rolling (or tilting) action of the forearm. Use but little weight, and you will have a true " passing-on " touch, the movement being due solely to the continuous rocking action of the Forearm, and the tone being but soft, flabby, and characterless. Keep the fingers together.

Next, instead of this unbroken rocking upon these two notes, give gentle but sufficiently strong *jerks* rotarily, alternately in each direction, so as to sound the notes sharply and definitely in a slow trill. Let the keys bounce up, and thus form *staccato*, while you nevertheless continue to rest on the surface of the Keyboard.

Having thus realized the true function and correct action of the function of Rotation, finally repeat these rotary jerks, but with the same fingers placed in their normal, separated position and condition, while accurately timing their individual action to correspond with each alternate rotary exertion. No better "finger individualization" exercise than this can be found, and it demonstrates in a moment that the only true solution of "finger individualization" is to be found in accurately coördinating and timing the action of the Rotation-muscles with that of the Finger-muscles and key-descent.

Note No. II.—ON REPEATED NOTES.

It is usually found "difficult" to repeat a note *with the same finger*, hence so much substituting of fingers on repeated notes. But the fault here again lies in the application of wrong rotary exertions. On repeating a note with the *same* finger (without any other finger intervening) the requirement is that we should, each time, *repeat the same* rotary exertion. Instead of this, we are tempted to make a *continuous* (rotary) exertion serve the purpose of the two (or more) repetitions required, hence the "stickiness."

Remember then, whenever you repeat a note with the same finger *without any other finger intervening*, you must repeat each time the same rotary exertion.

For instance, take the second Novellette of *Schumann's* in D major, unless you accurately *cease* and then repeat the rotary "jerk" towards the thumb, it is impossible to play the two successive **thumb-notes** with ease. The same rule applies even in the case of the *lower* note of the right hand passage of Chopin's Study in C major, No. 7, Op. 10, although the repeated note is here played alternately with thumb and index finger.

For the same reason, great care must be taken (rotatively) in playing octave passages, for in them one is apt to "set" the wrist — that is, to stiffen the rotary exertions one against the other. Take, for instance, the very light *quasi-glissando* octave passages of the Coda of the last movement of the "*Waldstein*" Sonata. It is a good plan to practise such a passage alternately either with the thumb alone, or with the *fifth* finger alone, keeping the hand in the meantime spread out, as if for the octave — although the octave-note is not here sounded. It will probably be found "difficult" thus to play the passage with the fifth finger alone. Again here, the " difficulty " (or rotary-fault, as a matter of fact) is at once conquered if you take care to *repeat* the rotary jerk in the same direction for each repeated note—each time towards the thumb if you are playing with the thumb alone, or each time towards the fifth finger if you are playing the passage with that alone. After such experiment, correctly done, the octave passage itself should prove quite easy.

It goes without saying, that it is here a question not of rotary *movements*, but of jerks or exertions, rotatively—exertions which you can apply perfectly well without even the slightest *visible* twisting of the arm. It is useful (however) at first to give an actual rotary movement for each note, so that the player may be enabled to realize the nature of the exertions required, and to ensure their being applied with perfect freedom.

Note No. III — ROTATION GYMNASTIC FOR THE FINGER ITSELF:

The following exercise is sometimes useful. Strictly speaking, this is not a Rotation Exercise, since it is not engendered by the Forearm muscles, but is an exercise of the lateral movements of the finger. It forms, however, one of the most effective Gymnastics available for freeing one's technique, for ensuring certainty in finding notes, and for attaining to subtlety in one's tone-shadings, and it therefore also forms an "individualization" study of first rank :—

On the edge of a table, etc., lightly rest with the tips of all the fingers, the fingers held *slightly* apart and perfectly "flat," so that an inch or more of the fleshy under-surface of each finger is in contact with the table.

Now, press slightly (very slightly) with *one* finger-tip, so as to obtain *sufficient* frictional adhesion upon the table surface, and then try to rotate that finger on itself. This, in reality, is impossible, but by exerting the finger laterally (alternately in each direction) the soft flesh will *give*, slightly, from side to side — the nail actually moving horizontally a quarter of an inch or so — and the finger will thus, as it were, actually revolve a small way in each direction; i. e., the finger will slightly "give" rotatively (twisting in its socket) owing to its lateral movement being restrained underneath by the friction of its flesh upon the table. Exercise each finger thus in turn, including the thumb. Use very little arm-weight in resting upon the table — the hand, loosely lying on the table, is almost sufficient weight.

Be careful to use no exertion save that of the finger itself; the operation is a most neat and delicate one when properly performed.

Besides being executed with "flat" finger, it may also be done "bent" finger, but the former is the better form of practice, as the whole is thus more likely to be done elastically, as it should be.

A somewhat related exercise can be performed at the keyboard.

Take the *extreme* extension group of arpeggio :*

Ex. 15.

Lento, ligato, egualemente   etc.

Play this *quite slowly*, and most delicately as to tone, resting with no more weight on the keyboard than will just suffice to retain each key depressed. Now, *as delicately and gently as possible rotate the forearm as far round as can comfortably be done* in sounding the successive notes of the arpeggio, always of course rolling the hand back to the opposite extreme position, before each successive note-taking.

We must here warn the student that this exercise is not only useless for its purpose but is really harmful, unless practised PERFECTLY GENTLY, as directed, and with full regard (full aural attention) to the actual sound of each note — a perfectly even and soft tone all the time.

* Those finding this full extension-group too severe, may employ the dominant-seventh group of five notes, as in Ex. 9, page 9.

Lowe and Brydone Printers Limited, London